NEWBERY HONOR-WINNING AUTHOR

JEAN ★ FRITZ

Who's saying what in Jamestown, Thomas Savage?

pictures by Sally Wern Comport

cover illustration by David Small

PUFFIN BOOKS
An Imprint of Penguin Group (USA) Inc.

PUFFIN BOOKS
Published by the Penguin Group
Penguin Young Readers Group, 345 Hudson Street, New York, New York 10014, U.S.A.
Penguin Group (Canada), 90 Eglinton Avenue East, Suite 700, Toronto, Ontario, Canada M4P 2Y3
(a division of Pearson Penguin Canada Inc.)
Penguin Books Ltd, 80 Strand, London WC2R 0RL, England
Penguin Ireland, 25 St Stephen's Green, Dublin 2, Ireland
(a division of Penguin Books Ltd)
Penguin Group (Australia), 250 Camberwell Road, Camberwell, Victoria 3124, Australia
(a division of Pearson Australia Group Pty Ltd)
Penguin Books India Pvt Ltd, 11 Community Centre, Panchsheel Park, New Delhi - 110 017, India
Penguin Group (NZ), 67 Apollo Drive, Rosedale, North Shore 0632, New Zealand
(a division of Pearson New Zealand Ltd.)
Penguin Books (South Africa) (Pty) Ltd, 24 Sturdee Avenue,
Rosebank, Johannesburg 2196, South Africa

Registered Offices: Penguin Books Ltd, 80 Strand, London WC2R 0RL, England

First published in the United States of America by G. P. Putnam's Sons, a division of Penguin Young Readers Group, 2007
Published by Puffin Books, a division of Penguin Young Readers Group, 2010

1 2 3 4 5 6 7 8 9 10

Text copyright © Jean Fritz, 2007
Interior illustrations copyright © Sally Wern Comport, 2007
Cover illustration copyright © David Small, 2010

THE LIBRARY OF CONGRESS HAS CATALOGED THE G. P. PUTNAM'S SONS EDITION AS FOLLOWS:
Fritz, Jean. Who's saying what in Jamestown, Thomas Savage? / Jean Fritz ; illustrations by Sally Wern Comport. p. cm.
1. Savage, Thomas, d. 1635—Juvenile literature. 2. Colonists—Virginia—Jamestown—Biography—Juvenile literature.
3. Jamestown (Va.)—History—17th century—Juvenile literature. 4. Jamestown (Va.)—Biography—Juvenile literature.
5. Virginia—History—Colonial period, ca. 1600–1775—Juvenile literature. I. Comport, Sally Wern. II. Title. III.
Title: Who is saying what in Jamestown, Thomas Savage?
F229.T56F75 2007   995.5'02092—dc22   [B   2006008260   ISBN 978-0-399-24644-9 (hc)

Puffin Books ISBN 978-0-14-241401-9

Printed in China

To the boys and girls of Virginia.

—J.F.

With a grateful spirit for having been
inspired by New Territory.

—S.W.C.

ACKNOWLEDGMENTS

Although it was frustrating not to find a record of Thomas's reactions to what was happening, I did meet a number of his descendants who couldn't give me the direct quotes I wanted, but who did encourage me to write this book. Jim Stewart of Winchester, Virginia, who first proposed Thomas as a subject to consider; Thomas Savage of Sotheby's in New York, who owns property on the Eastern Shore near the house of the first Thomas; Phillip Farrington Thomas, who has followed the adventures of the first Thomas closely as part of his study of his "extended family"; and Nancy Garrett, who has spent her life "living with Thomas Savage" on the Eastern Shore.

As I went ahead with the book, I became indebted to Curt Gaul of the National Park Service at Jamestown for his critical reading of the manuscript. And, as always, to my editor, Margaret Frith, who knows how to point out weaknesses while still maintaining confidence.

Finally, this book would not have been written without my daughter Andrea Pfleger, who took me to Jamestown for research, felt free to differ at times (which was always helpful), and who typed up the final manuscript.

—J. F.

FOREWORD

Why do I write biographies?

First: When I become interested in someone, I want to learn everything I can about that person.

Second: I want to share that person with you.

A biographer is expected to be nosy, so when I came to Thomas Savage, I tried to find out what he said, what he thought, what he felt.

But Thomas Savage didn't help me. He didn't keep a diary, for instance. If he did, he must have lost it. And I certainly never found it.

It might be enough just to tell all that happened to Thomas. And plenty did. After all, he was only thirteen when he became the first interpreter between the English and the Indians. He came through dangers and hardships and had many close calls, but did he complain? Not that I've heard of. Of course, he must have had many conversations with a variety of people, but what exactly did he say? Who knows?

But once I saw some of the tough situations that Thomas was up against, I found myself giving him words—enough so we'd get an idea of what it was like to settle in the New World when it was still new.

Without documentary evidence of what went on in Thomas's mind, I have to call this book historical fiction. Sometimes fiction can round out a story that might seem to get tight-lipped and skimpy without it. This is such a story.

Jean Fritz

CHAPTER 1

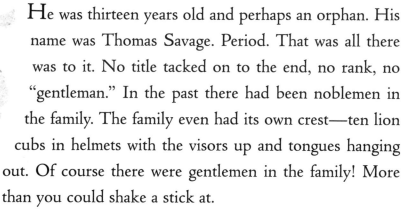

He was thirteen years old and perhaps an orphan. His name was Thomas Savage. Period. That was all there was to it. No title tacked on to the end, no rank, no "gentleman." In the past there had been noblemen in the family. The family even had its own crest—ten lion cubs in helmets with the visors up and tongues hanging out. Of course there were gentlemen in the family! More than you could shake a stick at.

To be a gentleman, a man had to own land, and Thomas, who was probably at the tail end of a large family, didn't inherit anything. He didn't own a square inch of land, not even of plain dirt. What could he look forward to? No land, no lions. Nothing—at least not in England. What he needed was a new country. And on the other side of the ocean, in the New World, there was one. America.

No one in Europe had even heard of America until 1492, and England had not paid much attention to it. But by 1606 they heard there was gold in one part of the New World—a lot of it. The Spanish had found it. So why not the English in their part of the New World? Besides, there were many spiders in this country, and everyone in those days knew that where there were spiders, there was gold.

So a group of businessmen in London formed what they called the Virginia Company, sent over three shiploads of settlers, and told them to build a city (to be known as Jamestown), and to hunt for gold. The next year they sent the first supply ship, the *John and Francis*, with more settlers, shovels, and food for everybody. Thomas Savage signed up to go on this ship. He couldn't put his name under the list of gentlemen passengers, so he did what he could. "Thomas Savage," he wrote. "Laborer."

When the ship sailed from England in late 1607, Thomas was not excited about finding gold; he didn't want to dig up his new country. He didn't talk about returning to England; he didn't plan to return. Virginia was to be his home. Meanwhile, he had to get used to a world of water— on all sides, day after day, month after month.

And as the captain's cabin boy, Thomas had to get used to the captain. Captain Christopher Newport was a kind man to work for, but there was the matter of his arm. Where there should have been a hand at the end of his left arm, there was a metal hook. Thomas tried not to stare, but wherever Captain Newport was, there was that hook. Thomas wondered how he had lost his hand, but Thomas didn't dare ask.

Besides, Captain Newport never had much to say. Not like the passengers who occupied the hold of the ship. These were the gentlemen and they had plenty to say. Nothing was right. The hold was crowded and in rough weather it stank of their vomit. They were knocked around, banging against each other and against the barrels of flour and kegs of oil that shared their quarters. Their voices were shrill, cussing out the weather, the ship, the Virginia Company, and America, which they hadn't even seen yet.

Did men always sound so mean, even in Jamestown? Thomas wanted to know. Captain Newport nodded. "Some of them."

Even with the Indians?

That was the trouble, Captain Newport explained. No one could talk with the Indians except Captain John Smith, and he was often away exploring. And here they were, Englishmen who were supposed to convert the Indians to Christianity so they could live together in peace. And all they could do was to talk with their hands or try to act out what they were saying! It was about this time that Captain Newport began calling Thomas "son."

Thomas would pick up another name in Jamestown. There, men called him "the little ensign." It was the lowest rank he could be given; it also meant he was the flag bearer in battle. Thomas didn't quite understand. Thomas knew that Indians fought behind trees, from tree to tree, so how could anyone carry a flag? As for the "little," Thomas was little, and even when he had his full growth, he was still little. So the name stuck.

It was the first week in January, 1608, when they finally reached Virginia, but Thomas didn't need to be told that this was land. Long before he could see it, the land proclaimed itself. The smell of loblolly pines and cedars drifted over the water while the air was alive with the high-pitched squabbling of birds looking for food, taking over the land-sea territory as their own. As the ship headed up the James River to the island where Jamestown was perched, Thomas squinted so that he would catch the first sight of people at the settlement. He knew that Captain Newport had left 104 men and boys behind

when he had sailed back to England. Thomas had often thought of the boys, wondering if he would make friends with them. Thomas could see the fort at one end of the island and a few houses, but no boys. Where was everybody? Why were there no welcoming shouts from the people of Jamestown?

Captain Newport was studying the empty landscape and frowning. As soon as the ship was tied safely to a tree onshore, he scrambled down the ladder to the ground, shouting a last-minute order that no one was to leave the ship. He was going to find Captain Smith and find out what was wrong.

Captain Smith was one of seven councilors appointed by the Virginia Company, but the other councilors (all gentlemen) did not like him. In his cocky bantam-rooster way, Captain Smith acted as if he knew everything. And he wasn't even a gentleman. Just a commoner, son of a yeoman farmer.

When Captain Newport came back, he looked so angry that Thomas knew the news was not good. "Captain Smith has been arrested," he said, "and they are going to hang him."

"What did he do?" Thomas asked.

"Nothing," Captain Newport snapped. "He had two men with him. When Captain Smith went onshore, he told the men to stay on the ship where they would be safe. They didn't. Indians found them and killed them. And so the people of Jamestown blame Captain Smith, even though he was, himself, captured by Indians and detained for weeks. They insist that the men from his ship who had been killed were Smith's responsibility."

"But it was the men's own fault," Thomas said. "They disobeyed. It doesn't make any sense."

"A lot of things that happen in Jamestown don't make sense," Captain

Newport admitted. "We got here just in time. I am a councilor in Jamestown too. I'll get Smith released."

And so he did. The next day he brought Captain Smith aboard the *John and Francis*. He was a short man with a huge red beard that looked as if it might catch fire from his anger. Captain Newport introduced Thomas.

"Are you all right?" Thomas asked. He felt timid. After all, he had never talked to a man who had just escaped hanging.

"Fine," Smith replied. "Thanks to this man here." He pointed at Captain Newport.

Thomas had one more question. Where was everyone?

John Smith did not waste words. "Dead," he said. At least most of them. Out of the 104 left here, only 38 had survived. For the most part, they either died from drinking dirty river water or they starved to death.

"Tufftaffety men," John Smith called them. Gentlemen too proud to get their hands dirty. They didn't know how to fish, farm or hunt. "They would rather," Smith said, "rot and die than do anything for themselves."

And *this* was where Thomas Savage was going to spend his life?

Captain Newport must have seen the shock on Thomas's face. "Would you rather live with the Indians?" he asked. Thomas didn't know. How could they be worse than the people in Jamestown? What were they like?

11

Captain Smith explained. All the Indians here were Algonquian, he said. The largest of the smaller local tribes in the area were Powhatans, ruled by their king Powhatan, who had taken his name from the tribe. He was the most powerful Indian. He was a big man and liked having his own way. Sometimes this meant he was strict; sometimes it meant he was cooperative. Judging by the food Smith ate during his captivity, a person who lived with the Indians would be better off than a person who lived in Jamestown, Smith said. At least he wouldn't go hungry.

Captain Newport turned from Captain Smith and Thomas to give orders to the sailors. He directed them to unload the ship, moving all the foodstuff they had brought to the storehouse.

For days Thomas joined in the work, until all at once the unloading stopped. Everything stopped. Jamestown was on fire! The flames spread quickly from one reed roof to another, to the fort, and yes, even to the storehouse. Thomas quickly found himself in a line of men filling bowls, pots and pitchers with river water to throw at the fire.

While working, Thomas was aware of strange people coming and going. Indians. Listening to them talk, Thomas was struck by their language. It was as if they had gathered all the sounds they could think of and strung them together to make long, awkward, deep-throated words. They sounded as if they were gargling, scraping syllables against each other.

All the struggle to stop the flames did little good. When the fire had finally burned itself out, Jamestown, as everyone could see, was reduced to ashes. Only one house had survived; most of the walls of the fort were damaged; the remaining houses had gone down along with the goods inside. Individuals began scraping through the ashes to find whatever remained. Some people had lost everything they owned—even their clothes (and this was winter!). Reverend Robert Hunt had lost his entire collection of fine books. Some people started moaning and complaining as they tried to make do; some kept it up for days. They wrote letters home, planning to give them to Captain Newport to deliver when he went back to England. "Send any old clothes you have," one wrote, "old underwear, coats, boots."

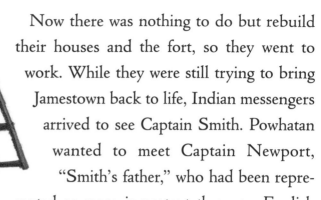

Now there was nothing to do but rebuild their houses and the fort, so they went to work. While they were still trying to bring Jamestown back to life, Indian messengers arrived to see Captain Smith. Powhatan wanted to meet Captain Newport, "Smith's father," who had been represented as more important than any English leader of Jamestown. The Indians understood that as Smith's "father," he was Smith's superior. If not a king, Newport was, in Indian thinking, close to a king.

Smith had realized this trip would be necessary and he had made plans for the boat trip up the river to Werowocomoco, Powhatan's town. As the two captains made preparations for the trip, Captain Newport turned to Thomas. "How would you like to go with us?" Of course, Thomas said yes.

"How would you like to stay there?" Newport went on. "Learn the language so you can help us understand the Indians."

"Stay?" Thomas repeated, as if the idea was too much to take in all at once. Live with the Indians? That was different.

Captain Smith liked the idea and obviously wanted to persuade Thomas. The Indian children seem happy, he said. You will have friends.

14

Thomas didn't answer immediately. Did he have a choice? After all, Captain Newport had made him cabin boy; he was used to telling Thomas what to do, as if he were a servant, or as if he were really a son. And Thomas was used to obeying. Finally he said yes, he would stay.

"You'll be better off," Captain Smith said. "If you return to Jamestown, you know what you will be doing? Digging for gold. Everyone in Jamestown has to dig. They *have* to find it. Captain Newport has promised to take gold back to England this time."

Thomas knew that on his previous trip, Newport had filled barrels with dirt that had gold specks in it. But was this gold? No, just ordinary dirt, as it turned out. Captain Newport and Captain Smith agreed on some things, but gold was not one of them. Captain Smith said no matter how many spiders they saw, there was no gold here. Captain Newport disagreed. Thomas didn't care either way. He packed his chest with what few clothes and belongings he had.

"There's just one thing, Thomas," Captain Smith added. "When you become an interpreter, you must not take sides. Just report the messages as they have been given to you. Even if it's hard, you must not comment."

It didn't sound hard to Thomas—not if he knew the language. Thomas resolved not to anticipate what Indian life would be like.

On the day they left, Captain Smith had with him gifts for Powhatan: a red suit, a hat, a bed and a white greyhound. "From King James," Smith explained. "Powhatan likes dogs."

As the ship pulled away, Thomas patted the dog. They had something in common. Neither of them would be coming back to Jamestown that trip.

When they reached Werowocomoco hours later, Captain Smith and the company of men who were to serve as guards debarked. But not Captain Newport, not Thomas. They were to stay on the ship out of sight until the next day. Smith wanted to make sure Powhatan was in a friendly mood for this visit.

The next day an English trumpeter stood by the ship as Newport and Thomas got off. As they approached Powhatan's long house in the village, the trumpeter gave them a marching tune. Thomas could not help but feel that this was an important occasion and he was part of the importance.

Inside the big house, children were sitting on the floor. Powhatan reportedly had twenty living sons and ten living daughters, including his favorite—Pocahontas. On one side of the room was a raised platform on which Powhatan's wives sat—at least ten of them. Then coming down from the platform to greet his guests was Powhatan himself. Thomas would have known he was the king; anyone would know it. He stood like a king, walked like a king, and even if you didn't understand him, he talked like a king. But not a king like King James I of England, who was skinny and small and, as everyone said, spilled his food down the front of his clothes.

Powhatan went back on his platform, and with Captain Smith interpreting, he and Newport were exchanging what Smith called "pretty talk." Then suddenly Captain Newport became serious. He put his hand on Thomas's shoulder.

"This is my son, Thomas," he said, "and I hereby give him to you as proof of our friendship. He will learn your language and I hope will serve you well."

Thomas found himself swallowing hard. "Give," Captain Newport had said, as if he were another greyhound! How could you *give* a person?

Captain Smith nodded at Thomas as if he were saying: This was all right. This was the Indian way. He, too, had been adopted by Powhatan.

In return, Powhatan gave Captain Newport a young brave for him to take to England. During the long afternoon of conversation between the two captains and Powhatan, Thomas squatted beside Newport. Then all at once it was time for the two captains to go back to the river and return to Jamestown.

Thomas, accompanied by what must have been an Indian guard, went with them to the water. As Thomas watched the ship pull into the middle of the river, he must have felt alone. More alone that he'd ever felt in his life. The forest behind him enclosed the world in darkness. And there he was.

He realized then that actually he wasn't alone. Dozens of young children had followed him and were surrounding him. They were feeling his clothes, touching the white skin of his hands and arms.

"Thomas Newport," they chanted as they danced around him. "Thomas Newport. Thomas Newport."

So, Thomas had another name. He didn't mind, particularly if only children used it. He was tired of people making a joke of his real name.

"Savage?" they would say. "A Savage going to live with other savages!"

The English had a habit of referring to people who were not Christian as "savages." Of course, the Indians took offense. So did Thomas.

CHAPTER 2

Determined to do a good job, Thomas concentrated on the language, listening and questioning. Pocahontas, interested in all Englishmen, had soon made friends with Thomas. When she couldn't find Captain Smith, who was her favorite, she spent time with Thomas. At first, Thomas found it hard to look directly at Pocahontas, just as he had once found it hard to look at Captain Newport and his hook. Pocahontas was naked. Even when she was showing off how well she did cartwheels. But Thomas quickly got over his discomfort when he realized that she was only following Indian custom. What was strange about that? Pocahontas must have been about eleven, and in another year or so, she would be twelve. Then, like all Indian girls, she would tie a deerskin apron around her waist. Her naked days would be over.

Whenever he saw Pocahontas, Thomas would greet her as he did all Indians: "Wingapo," he would say. Then he would ask her for Indian words. He'd point to a tree or to the river and she would tell him the word, but she didn't like his pointing. She wanted him to ask her properly, so she taught him. "Kaka torawincs?" Which meant, "What do you call this?"

By this time, Thomas found he could understand much of what was said, but speak? It was hard to wrap his mouth around words that sounded like pebbles rattling around on the bottom of a creek. Still, he didn't have to speak yet.

As winter slowly wore away to spring, Thomas was feeling more at home with the Indians. Compared to Jamestown, where the colonists were always complaining and arguing, Werowocomoco was a happy place.

It was about this time that Powhatan gave Thomas his first job. He was to take a message to Captain Newport, who was leaving for England in a few days. He should tell Newport that Powhatan would give him twenty turkeys in exchange for twenty swords.

Thomas wasted no time leaving for the six-hour walk to Jamestown. When he arrived, he went straight to Newport and recited his message.

Newport smiled. "Tell Powhatan that as soon as I receive the turkeys, I'll send the swords." He studied Thomas. "How do you like living with the Indians, Thomas?"

"Fine." As soon as he spoke, he knew what he had said was true, but he knew he shouldn't comment or make a social occasion of his business trips.

"Well," the captain went on, "if Jamestown succeeds, you'll be part of its success."

If? What did he mean—*if?* He hadn't come to Jamestown just to watch it vanish, the way the colony of Roanoke had vanished twenty years ago.

Powhatan waited until after Newport had left for England, then he told Thomas to return to Jamestown and give the same message to Captain Smith. Twenty more turkeys for twenty more swords.

Thomas knew that this wasn't likely to work. Trade was another matter about which the two captains disagreed. Newport thought that if you gave the Indians what they asked for, they would want to keep the peace. Smith thought that if you were not tough, the Indians would take advantage. Besides, Smith was against giving the Indians any English weapons.

Thomas, however, did as he was told, setting out on his long walk to Jamestown. In daylight, Thomas never felt alone in the quiet Virginia wilderness. There were too many wild things around. Sometimes there would be a flock of passenger pigeons traveling overhead, sometimes blocking out the sun. Sometimes there would be a flying squirrel or an eagle. Or there might be a wolf or a wildcat skulking in the undergrowth. Thomas would finger his bow and arrow that he'd been carrying ever since he had learned how to use them.

Often a bird with gray feathers would swoop down to greet him. Landing on a branch above Thomas, it would twitch its tail and sing. Thomas wouldn't have known that this was a mockingbird, able to imitate any bird in the forest. To Thomas it was always his little interpreter bird.

At Jamestown, Thomas found Captain Smith working with a pile of broken tools. The captain picked up a couple of broken shovels. "Look at this," he said in disgust. "See what gold digging did."

Thomas knew that gold still had not been found. No matter how many spiders there were, Thomas didn't believe that gold would be found, but he was not here to talk about gold. He had a message from Powhatan, he said. He delivered the message just as he had to Captain Newport.

Captain Smith, his beard bristling, threw the shovels down. "And he calls that a bargain, does he? Turkeys for the English to eat, swords to kill them. I'm not such a fool. Never! Tell Powhatan that I say never!" Then Smith added a request to his reply. Would Powhatan please send a guide to take him on a trip he'd soon be making? Not any guide. Captain Smith named a specific man. Thomas knew this man. He was one of Powhatan's leaders who would never be asked to do such a trifling job that boys usually did.

Back at Werowocomoco, Thomas tried to find softer words to convey Captain Smith's message because he knew Powhatan would not like it. But there was no way to soften it.

And yes, Powhatan was angry, just as Thomas expected. His face twisted in scorn; he looked as if he were about to break into a war dance, stamping his feet, shouting his hullabaloos.

"And Smith calls Captain Newport his father?" Powhatan cried. "But he won't send me swords as his father did. What kind of man is that?" He took a deep breath; more anger was coming. "He refuses to do me a favor, but asks for one of my top men to act as his guide, a boy's job." He suddenly turned on Thomas.

"And you!" he snarled. "Get your chest, take your English clothes and get out! Tell them at Jamestown to send me another boy."

Thomas left. He put the chest on one shoulder and started the long walk back. He was a failure. The words kept repeating themselves with every heavy footstep. The chest dug into his shoulder. What other boys were there in Jamestown? They were all servants or laborers. He didn't want to be either.

It seemed so easy in this country to give a person away as a gift and just as easy to throw him away.

Of course, he was downhearted when he reached Jamestown. All the people he saw at Jamestown were, as usual, miserable and discouraged.

Then, to Thomas's surprise, the guide whom Smith had requested arrived. But, after a few days, he mysteriously disappeared before Smith left on his trip. It was obvious to Thomas that Powhatan had told him to do this.

Powhatan wasn't ready to forgive Captain Smith for refusing his bargain. In retaliation, he told his men to steal whatever swords they could. And not only swords, but also armor of any kind. And tools. If this required killing Englishmen, then kill. In turn, when the English caught the Indians stealing, they made them prisoners—thirteen before they finished. (The Indians captured two English.)

Could this be settled? Powhatan sent Indian representatives to ask for the release of the Indian prisoners. In return, Powhatan offered to set free their two English prisoners.

"Thirteen for two?" the English asked. Not a fair trade. Finally, when Powhatan sent a group of Indians along with his daughter Pocahontas to ask for the prisoners, the colonists agreed to the exchange. But first, the Indian prisoners had to go to church in the hope that this might turn them into Christians. They were marched into the little church on the grounds of the fort. They were told to do what the English did. They stood up and knelt down—up and down, up and down. They brushed their hands across their chests when the English crossed themselves.

When they walked back to Werowocomoco, Thomas went with them, at Pocahontas's special request. Her father, she said, loved Thomas very much.

No one had started to look for Captain Newport's return yet; in April 1608 the *Phoenix* arrived, commanded by Captain Francis Nelson.

Five months later, in September, Captain Newport came and with him were four important directives from the Virginia Company to Jamestown.

1. They should find a shortcut to the Pacific Ocean (they called it the South Sea) which would take them to China.

2. At the very least they should find something that would make a profit

for England. They hadn't found any gold. They had tried silkworms for spinning fine silk cloth, but no luck there.

3. They were to search for survivors of the Roanoke Colony. No luck there either.

4. They were to hold a coronation ceremony and put a crown on Powhatan's head to make him a vassal king under King James.

This last order caused the greatest controversy. Captain Newport thought it was a great idea and so did many of the men in Jamestown. Captain Smith thought it was ridiculous. This would just make Powhatan so puffed up with importance that he'd demand more and more for his corn. Right away Thomas would have known this was not a good idea. He would have known that Powhatan would have to kneel for the crown, and that Powhatan would find this humiliating.

Captain Newport sent a message to Powhatan, inviting him to Jamestown to receive gifts from King James. Powhatan refused.

"If your king has sent me presents, I also am a king and this is my land. Your father (Newport) is to come to me, not I to him, nor will I bite at such a bait."

The English accepted this change and they got ready to go to Werowocomoco. Newport sent Powhatan's gifts by boat: a wash basin, a pitcher, a scarlet cloak, a pair of shoes for a man who normally wore moccasins, and the crown. Newport, with a party of thirty men, traveled by foot.

When it came time for the coronation, however, neither Newport nor Thomas could get Powhatan to understand what was expected. The English employed body language—pretending to kneel, pretending to put on a crown. Powhatan looked blank. Captain Newport himself demonstrated kneeling. So did Thomas. All the English were bobbing up and down while Powhatan stared into the distance. Thomas knew it would be like this. He closed his eyes.

Finally, one Englishman leaned heavily on Powhatan's shoulders until, in spite of himself, he bent over. The crown was quickly clapped on his head. A gun was fired into the air. From the boat, anchored in the river, came the booming of cannon. The ceremony was over.

Powhatan apparently decided to give gifts too—old ones would be all right. He had an old deerskin cloak and an old pair of moccasins. He handed them to Captain Newport.

Now spring was here. Thomas had come to love Indian ceremonies, but his favorite was "Planting Time in the Spring." A special day was set for the planting of the king's crop and the Indian townspeople came early—men and women and children. They set out corn, beans, peas, gourds and other seeds in a large field of about one hundred acres. They finished their work in a day. The next day was for the celebration, with Powhatan himself as the center of it. Powhatan took his place at one end of the field with all the planting people lined up, facing him. First an attendant handed Powhatan what he was to wear for the occasion.

Watching from one side of the field, Thomas drew in his breath. Powhatan was putting on King James's crown that he had recently refused so rigorously. Thomas supposed he'd never see that crown again, but here was Powhatan wearing it with evident pride as he began the long walk around his planted field. He walked backward, reaching into a big bowl of beads that an attendant was carrying at his side. He would throw a handful of the beads in the direction of the people who followed him. They would stoop, scrambling for the beads, amid shouts of glee. Everyone was obviously having a good

time and no one more than Powhatan. His crown slightly askew, he was joking, calling out to friends among his followers. For a moment Thomas almost wished he were an Indian, but he chased that thought away. He must never forget he was English and proud of it.

As Powhatan backed past Thomas, he leaned over and pressed a bead in his hand. Thomas closed his hand around it. He knew the bead had no value, but he knew he'd keep this bead always.

Back in Jamestown, Captain Newport was getting ready to return to England. He knew he wouldn't be back for six or seven months.

Could the English survive that long? They were not doing well. Not even the leaders were doing well. Two councilors had drowned when their skiff had turned over. Another councilman (George Kendall) had been arrested, tried for mutiny and shot. The first president, Edward Wingfield, had been deposed, accused of living off his private supply of food while the colony starved. John Ratcliffe became the second president, but Thomas did not think that he would last long. He demanded that Jamestown build him a palace in the woods. Of course, everyone turned against him. Thomas secretly hoped that Captain Smith would be the next president. He would turn Jamestown into a normal city. He wouldn't stand for laziness. Or craziness.

Soon Ratcliffe was sent back to England, and John Smith did become president on September 10, 1608. And just as Thomas had hoped, John Smith set about improving Jamestown. He made strict laws. Anyone who didn't work would not be allowed to eat. Anyone who swore would have cold water poured down his arm.

Jamestown's most critical problem was, as usual, shortage of food, and there would soon be more mouths to feed. Captain Newport and the third supply would be bringing more colonists.

On August 11, 1609, a year after Smith became president, the first four ships of an eight-ship flotilla that made up the third supply arrived. A few days later three others pulled up in Jamestown.

But not the flagship. It had not yet arrived. The people ran down to the water to get news from the new ships. "What news?" people shouted. "What have you got on board?"

"Three hundred new colonists," was the answer.

Three hundred! The people groaned. Where would they put them? What would they eat?

"One of our newcomers is named Ratcliffe," the voice from the ship continued. "He seems to know this place."

Ratcliffe! Does he expect us to finish his palace?

The voice from the deck went on, "You'll have a new governor. He'll come later on the flagship."

"Where is the flagship?"

"It'll be along one of these days."

The flagship, however, didn't come and didn't come. Captain Newport was on the flagship as well as the new governor, Sir Thomas Gates, with a new charter. How could the Virginia Company have allowed the people important to the colony and the charter to be together on the same ship?

Captain Smith would have said it was typical. What could he do with 300 new colonists? He couldn't stuff them all into the fort, so he would do what the Indians did when short of food. He'd send the newcomers in groups into the surrounding area to feed off the land.

The newcomers did not care for this plan at all. They had come to the New World expecting to find gold, but all they found was trouble. Indians who already lived on this land to which the newcomers had been assigned didn't want to move to a new village. The newcomers didn't want to live in the Indians' old houses, but neither had a choice.

Captain Smith went to see the difficulties between these new colonists and the Indians for himself. He took with him a newcomer, young Henry Spelman, who, he thought, might be a help. Henry seemed to get along with Parahunt, son of Powhatan, so Smith decided to leave him there to get acquainted.

Before Smith left, he "sold" Henry to the Indians. Henry didn't understand the Indian language, so he didn't know why he had been sold, and it was not until later that he learned he was to be an interpreter-in-training.

Henry was still there when fighting began among the Indians, so Henry decided he was acquainted enough. He rushed to get on the ship anchored in the river and returned to Jamestown.

As it happened, Thomas Savage was also in Jamestown, delivering some venison to George Percy, who was rumored to be the temporary president until the flagship arrived. The flagship had been so delayed, however, that everyone had stopped looking for it. John Smith did not agree to Percy as temporary president. He hadn't completed his own term of office, he said; he'd stay until he had.

Once Thomas had delivered the venison, his errand was done and he knew he should return to Powhatan, yet he hesitated. It was a long walk and the woods were dark and filled with Indians on the prowl. He wished, he said, he had a "countryman" to go with him. Henry was appointed. Thomas had heard of Henry, who he hoped would become a friend. But Henry was a young gentleman and you could never tell about gentlemen.

"How do you like Virginia?" Henry asked as they started out.

It was a good country, Thomas replied. As long as a person stayed away from Jamestown. Henry knew that he would eventually be an interpreter like Thomas. "Do they expect us to keep the peace?" he asked.

Thomas wasn't sure that anyone could keep the peace.

As they walked along, a bird burst into song. Thomas laughed and whistled back. "He's like a friend," he told Henry. He explained that this bird could speak the language of every bird in the woods. He thought of him as an interpreter.

"May I speak to him too?" Henry asked.

Of course. The business of being a gentleman was not going to get in the way at all.

CHAPTER 3

Henry stayed with Thomas for
about a month, during which time
Powhatan made him welcome. At every
meal, he invited both boys to eat with him,
even once while entertaining a visitor, the king
of the Patawomekes on the Potomac River.

But where was John Smith?

When he left Henry, he had started back to
Jamestown, just as he had planned, but he had second
thoughts. He wasn't happy with the way things were going with the new
colonists and the Indians in the settlement. So he returned again, but when
the situation had not improved, John Smith left for Jamestown in disgust.

Climbing in the boat with his friends, he lay down on the bottom. He was
tired; it had been a long day and there were more than seventy miles to cover
before they reached the colony. He had some gunpowder in a bag on his hip,
but he didn't give it a thought. Until a spark, perhaps from a pipe of one of
his friends, dropped on the gunpowder bag.

The bag burst into flame!

Captain Smith was afire! Instinctively he jumped into the water. The fire
went out, but the burn was so serious and so painful, he couldn't get back into
the boat. His friends managed to pull him in and rowed as fast as they could
to Jamestown. His trousers had a huge hole above the gunpowder bag, so the

burn was obvious—about ten inches square with the skin and flesh gone.

In order to heal, Smith knew he would need more care than he could get in Jamestown. He was carried to his quarters and made arrangements to leave for England on the next ship. He told his friends who had been with him, "Tell the Indians I am dead."

The news traveled swiftly up and down the river, but when the Indians heard it, they heard Smith's own version. Captain Smith was dead. Pocahontas went to Jamestown. "Where is Captain Smith?" she asked.

They told her just what they had told the other Indians. "Dead," they said.

Pocahontas could not bear to stay where John Smith had once been, but was no longer. She took off for the Potomac country where she had friends.

Powhatan made new plans. Captain Smith was his most dangerous adversary. With him out of the way, Powhatan could put all his energy into getting rid of the English. He could kill and he could starve. He would do both.

He instructed the Indians living nearby (many of whom were his vassals) to refuse to trade with the English. He told his own warriors to kill any English venturing out of their fort even for a few minutes. This winter— 1609–1610—came to be known as the Starving Time.

It soon became obvious that this was not just harassment that Powhatan was inflicting; it was war. Bodies of dead English were repeatedly found in the woods. Once a whole group was discovered, their mouths stuffed with corn—the Indians' show of contempt for a people who could not feed themselves.

Then suddenly, without explanation, Powhatan did something that seemed entirely out of character to Thomas. He sent Henry to Old Point Comfort, an outpost at the tip of the James River and Chesapeake Bay, where Ratcliffe was stationed, and told Henry to invite Ratcliffe and a group of his men to come to his capital at Orepakes and trade. Thomas could not believe this. What was the point of starving the colonists and, at the same time, extending this invitation to trade?

Ratcliffe, however, was overwhelmed. He imagined himself becoming an instant hero when he returned to Jamestown with a boatload of corn! He loaded a barge with sixty men and off they went. He expected everything to go smoothly, but right from the beginning the English made mistakes.

Normally before trading, the two sides agreed to exchange hostages as proof of their honesty and their good intentions. Ratcliffe ignored this custom entirely. Later in the storehouse, after most of the trading had been accomplished, some of Ratcliffe's men accused the Indians of making false bottoms in the baskets for corn so that the baskets would appear to be fuller than they were. The Indians didn't like these accusations. In retaliation, they lay in the tall grass where the English would have to pass on their way to their boats. The Indians aimed their arrows at the English. Thirty colonists were killed.

There was more. The women of the town grabbed Captain Ratcliffe, tied him to a burning tree and with sharpened shells began cutting off every appendage of his body. Sometimes they threw the body piece in Ratcliffe's face, sometimes directly into the fire. In the end, they took mussel shells and scraped all the skin from his body.

Powhatan led his wives and Henry away from the killing scene. Thomas, who apparently stayed, was forced at times to cover his ears and eyes to avoid what he saw and heard. Even Ratcliffe, he thought, didn't deserve such cruelty.

Henry worried if Jamestown would blame him for having a part in this.

"Do you think the Indians did this on their own, or was it planned in advance?" Henry asked Thomas later.

Thomas shook his head. It sounded planned. He reminded Henry of the way the people in Jamestown referred to Powhatan—"the subtle (secretive) old fox." He could have arranged it.

After sharing his worries with Thomas, Henry had a suggestion. They could follow the king of Patawomekes, who was visiting, when he left. He had liked the boys; perhaps he would invite them to stay with him. So then Henry would avoid any accusations.

The two boys left, along with a German boy named Samuel who had been staying with Powhatan. Samuel had come to the colony to help make glass, but had not been able to decide where his loyalties lay. The three kept well behind the departing king, but they had not gone far when Thomas began to question what he was doing. *Stop*, he told himself. *Think*. Do you want to continue? *No*, he admitted. *Then turn around*. At a moment when the other two were not looking his way, Thomas turned around and headed back to Powhatan. How could he desert Powhatan? he asked. Powhatan thought of him as a son. And, after all, he had no part in this business. Besides, if he ran away, who would trust him again?

As soon as he was back on familiar Indian territory, Thomas tried to avoid Powhatan, but Powhatan was looking for him. He had questions to ask Thomas. When he heard what had happened, Powhatan sent several of his warriors to intercept the other boys. When he found them, he ordered them to stop. When they didn't, the warrior took a hatchet and buried it in the German boy's head. He would have done the same with Henry, but Henry was already escaping. He "shifted for himself" and continued his journey to the Potomac country. On his arrival, he was placed with Japazeus, chief of a town, and became a close member of the family. He would brag that no one could keep Japazeus's baby as quiet as he could.

Everyone now realized that Powhatan was at war. The men stationed at the English outposts, afraid for their safety, rushed to Jamestown.

Thomas was not one of the early ones to flee to Jamestown, but he did go. There was no need to know the Indian language now. No one was talking. He felt sad, but he knew he was not deserting Powhatan. By fighting the English, Powhatan had deserted him.

When Thomas got to Jamestown, he could hardly believe the condition of the place. People were not only starving, they looked defeated. Doors had been taken down to be used as firewood; bones of animals and trash littered the floors. The gates of the fort were partly open, its lock broken. And George Percy, the temporary president, sat in his satin coat and new shoes before his table set with English silver. He was one of those who believed that English gentlemen should follow English customs, no matter where they were. Thomas knew that the Jamestown settlers had only been allotted one half a cup of gruel a day and a small portion of wormy peas. They had resorted to eating dogs and cats, rats and mice, and snakes if they could catch them. What did President Percy do? Thomas wondered. Did he use his silver knife and fork on a mouse? And look at the ruff around his neck. It stood up straight and stiff, not like the other ruffs here, which were limp—all because it had been discovered that the starch that was used to keep the ruffs in shape was edible and tasted better than the gruel.

Thomas knew that the Indians hated him as much as they hated the other English. He could hear them singing. "Thomas Newport. Thomas Newport," they sang. "We will do our best to wound or kill you despite your bright sword."

On March 10, 1610, six months after Captain Smith's departure, only sixty colonists out of five hundred in Jamestown were still surviving.

On March 24 (May 23, 1610, according to the New Style calendar), two little ships, the *Patience* and the *Deliverance*, sailed into Jamestown. The passengers debarked, led by Sir Thomas Gates, the new president of the colony. They entered the forlorn shambles of the fort, which was obviously deserted.

By instinct, Thomas Gates went directly to the church still standing in the center of the fort and ordered someone to ring the bells.

Out of their houses struggled those men who could still walk. *Were these the men from the missing flagship?* they wondered. Not daring to believe, but hoping that help had finally arrived, they gathered to ask questions.

The new arrivals explained that the flagship, the *Sea Venture*, had encountered a tempest and had been stranded on the Bermuda Islands. They told the remarkable story of how they had built the ships that had carried them here.

No need for the colonists to tell their story. Thomas Gates and his men could see for themselves the terrible condition of Jamestown.

The question was: "Now what?"

Thomas Gates revealed they had enough food to last for only a couple of weeks. He looked at the skeleton-like figures of the colonists and at the havoc in their town. He admitted that they would probably have to turn around and go back to England.

There was a moment of silence; then a cheer went up from the long-suffering survivors.

On the morning of June 7, the settlers lined up to board the ships to which they had been assigned. The cannon of the fort had been buried outside the gates; the fort itself had guards stationed at strategic intervals to prevent fires, which enthusiastic settlers had threatened to set. Still, there was no quelling the enthusiasm. In the background, a drum beat a slow, mournful march as if it were a funeral, but not loud enough to cover the happy shouts of those departing for England.

Thomas wished the happy settlers would hush up. This was not a happy time. That drum was playing a dirge for England itself that had lost this colony that they had tried to build in the New World. As for Thomas, that drum was playing a final farewell to his own dreams of living out his life in this new home with Indians as neighbors. He looked out at the land around Jamestown. He knew that Powhatan's Indians were hiding in the tall grass, congratulating themselves on winning the war, glad to see the English leaving the country to them.

Thomas would have liked to raise a hand in greeting, but they would only have picked him out as a target. He followed the other colonists. He was sixteen and here he was leaving a country that he had counted on as being his home. And who here would miss him? Maybe Henry if he heard what had happened. Maybe Pocahontas if she knew. Maybe the little bird who had recently been trying to imitate his whistle.

CHAPTER 4

Two of the ships that had transported the colonists to Virginia had stayed behind. They joined the two from Bermuda sailing down the James River. They went about ten miles and anchored at Hog Island, which had once held the hogs they had brought from England, but was deserted now, since the Indians had slaughtered them.

The next morning they started off again, leaving Jamestown and all the little patches of land behind. The river, as it opened up in front of them, seemed endless and empty until a ship appeared on the horizon, making its way toward them. A man stood on the deck of the approaching ship, waving a paper, shouting something into the wind. The words were finally clear. "Sir Thomas Gates," he called, "Sir Thomas Gates."

One way or another, he eventually was able to get the paper into Sir Thomas Gates' hands. Gates read the message, called all the passengers to their forward decks, and gave them the news.

Following behind the ship with its message were more ships. Lord Delaware was on the way. He was the new governor of Virginia, appointed for life. He had with him 150 new settlers and a year's supply of food. He ordered those who were leaving Jamestown to turn around and go back.

The arrival of a hurricane could not have caused more anguish. Yet it was quiet, deathly quiet, as the four little ships tacked into a reverse course and headed back up the river. Thomas may have been the only one whose heart lifted at Lord Delaware's orders.

What would they find? Thomas wondered. Had the Indians taken over the fort? Would they still be as hostile?

Everything was just as they had left it. Indeed, when Lord Delaware finally came ashore, he covered his nose with his handkerchief. The stench from those who had died, from those who had been sick and from the garbage and filth was overwhelming. Lord Delaware told the settlers to clean up the fort, throw everything into a pit and cover it up. He would sleep on the ship.

What about the Indians? Thomas wondered. Would they have changed?

The answer was *no*. The sniping, the harassing, the taunting continued as usual. The difference was that people could eat. Even with all the new supplies, however, there was no fresh food—no meat, no corn.

They managed as they could, but in 1613 they asked Captain Samuel Argall, who had just been appointed admiral of Virginia to replace Captain Newport, to inspect the eastern seashore for possible harbors. After that, he was told to go to the Potomac country in search of food. There was obviously no hope of anything from the Powhatan Indians. He would need an interpreter, so Thomas Savage was assigned to him, at least for the first part of his trip.

This was Thomas's introduction to the Eastern Shore, and he fell in love with it. First, the whole peninsula seemed almost deliberately to have distanced itself from the mainland and Jamestown. Then there was always a plentiful supply of seafood—mussels, oysters, crabs, all kinds of shellfish, in addition to ocean fish. But most important were the people, members of the Accawmacke tribe, who, although subjects of Powhatan, acted independently. Rather than being suspicious of the English, they treated them as they treated all strangers: as guests—an attitude that was undoubtedly encouraged by their king, Debedeavon (commonly called "the Laughing King").

Although there is no record of Thomas accompanying Captain Argall when he went north on his trading mission, it is hard not to picture him there. We know Thomas was with Argall on the Eastern Shore and it is possible he stayed when Argall turned north to the Potomac country. But if he had been there, he would have, like Argall, heard that Pocahontas was visiting nearby. And he would have known of Argall's plan to kidnap her. Why? Thomas might have asked. Because this was how the people of Jamestown could get back all the guns and swords that Powhatan had stolen from them, and the prisoners he had taken. These could serve as ransom.

Accordingly, Argall asked Japazeus, the local chieftain, and his wife to lure Pocahontas on board his boat; he would manage from there. It worked out perfectly, just as Argall had planned it. When Japazeus and his wife were leaving the boat after their visit, Argall told Pocahontas that she was staying on board. Of course, she realized then what was happening, but Argall reassured her. She would be fine, he said. Her father would soon claim her. If Thomas were there, he too would have tried to comfort her. He might have told her what she wanted to hear: Captain Smith might still be alive. Would she have believed him?

"Your people lie much," she once said.

When they got to Jamestown, Argall sent a message to Powhatan, telling him of the ransom. The English had tried once before to get the guns and swords back and to have the prisoners freed. Delaware, who had been sick most of his stay in Virginia, had returned to England. Sir Thomas Dale was in charge now and he told Powhatan that if he complied with the ransom demands, he would be a friend of Dale's. King James would be his friend too. Powhatan laughed at such arrogance. It was *his* friendship the English should be seeking.

Powhatan did free his captives. In addition, he sent a handful of tools and a few broken guns. That was all he had, he insisted. The rest had been lost or stolen.

Not satisfactory, the English said. Pocahontas was scornful. Her father did not value her as much as his old guns and axes. She would continue to be held by the English.

She had her reasons. While with the English, she had been learning about Christianity from Alexander Whitaker, a minister from Cambridge;

she also had another tutor. John Rolfe, a Bermuda survivor, was making it a habit of calling on her when he had finished his daily farmwork. Rolfe, who had always been a smoker, didn't care for the tobacco the Indians used, so he was experimenting with tobacco plants from the Caribbean.

However proper their conversation, Pocahontas and Rolfe fell in love. After Pocahontas was baptized and after Rolfe had received permission from Sir Thomas Dale, the acting governor, the two were married in April 1614. Thomas, now twenty and acting as interpreter for Ralph Hamor, an investor and large landholder in Virginia, attended the ceremony. As he watched the amazing alliance of an Englishman and an Indian, he may have hoped, like everyone else, that this might mean peace. And it did. Indeed, the period that followed has been called "The Peace of Pocahontas." The English and Indians of the colony lived beside each other in harmony—even in friendship.

The wedding of Rolfe and Pocahontas was such a gala affair that it gave Sir Thomas Dale ideas. If one wedding was such a success, why not two weddings? He'd had his eye on Powhatan's youngest daughter, who, though not quite twelve, was a beauty. He asked Ralph Hamor to deliver a letter to Powhatan with his proposal. Thomas Savage accompanied Hamor as interpreter, uneasy about how Powhatan would receive him. After all, he knew that Powhatan had been especially angry with him throughout the recent hostilities. He entered, almost hesitantly, to face Powhatan, but to his surprise Powhatan addressed him immediately.

"My child," he said in his booming voice, "you are welcome. You have been a stranger to me these four years. What time I gave you leave to go (to) Jamestown to see your friends, till now, you never returned. You are my child by the donative (gift) of Captain Newport."

Thomas had missed the friendship of Powhatan. He put his hand over his heart to indicate his pleasure at being back in Powhatan's good graces.

Looking at Powhatan for the first time in so long, Thomas couldn't help but notice how Powhatan had aged. His face had softened; he seemed to move more slowly. He was still every inch a king, but Thomas thought he wouldn't be a king much longer.

Thomas turned his attention back to the business of the moment. It was hard to picture Sir Thomas Dale wooing a twelve-year-old when, as everyone knew, he had a wife at home waiting for him. He was one of the many governors of the colony since Lord Delaware, who, after only a year in Virginia, had taken sick and returned to England. Of all of them, Dale was the harshest. The settlers knew that just one false step meant punishment, if not death. And now here Dale was, begging for the hand of Powhatan's daughter.

This daughter, Powhatan replied, had been promised to another. And she was already three days away.

Could he not recall her? Hamor asked. After all, Sir Thomas Dale wanted only to ensure the peace between the two people.

"He (Dale) should not need to distrust any injury from me," Powhatan said. "There have already been too many of his men and mine killed, and by my occasion there should never be more."

Dale did not get the young wife he had asked for, but he did get Powhatan's promise of peace.

In the years following, the colony of Jamestown experienced more stability than it ever had. Indians dropped in at English homes at their pleasure, staying for supper if they were invited. Governor Wyatt, new to Virginia, wrote that he found the colony "in great amity and confidence with the natives." By 1618 the colony had a population of 1,000. There were now four small communities, some having started as outposts. In addition to Jamestown, there were Henricus, Elizabeth City, and Charles City. Plantations appeared up and down the James River—all of them large in order to take care of the tobacco that everyone was raising.

Indeed, the Virginia Company had never stopped ordering the colony to find or develop some product that would be of value to the Mother Country. They had, of course, made various experiments, but tobacco turned out to be the answer. John Rolfe was successful with his experiment and his tobacco was popular with everyone—Indians, colonists, English in England—particularly young men who puffed tobacco smoke from one end of the country to the other. But not King James. He made a face every time he smelled tobacco or even when he heard the word mentioned. Still, he did like the money.

In 1619, the government of the colony changed. In place of the charter they had been living under, the Virginia Company gave them what was called "The Great Charter." The members of the Virginia assembly (the House of Burgesses) were to be elected by "freemen." Servants could not vote in England, but they could in Virginia. Democracy was being introduced, and after eight years of martial law, English common law was reinstated in Virginia.

As always in any population, people die, people rise and people fall.

In 1616 Pocahontas went to England for a visit with her husband; she died in 1617 on her way home.

A year later Powhatan died, unhappy over Pocahontas's death, discouraged by the defection of certain of his allies.

The next in line of succession was Opitchapam, the older of Powhatan's two brothers, but Opitchapam was sickly and didn't look a bit like a king. The next brother was Opechancanough, who not only looked and acted like a king, but wanted to be one. He let Opitchapam keep the title, but he began to rule. He was not one to take halfway measures, as he blamed Powhatan for doing, but who knew what he was really up to?

There were three interpreters now. Henry Spelman had returned from England and was back with his Potomac Indians. Robert Poole, a newcomer, was a little older than the other two and was assigned to live with Opechancanough. No one really trusted Robert, as he seemed to work for both sides and neither side; Thomas felt sorry for him, stuck with Opechancanough, who hated all Englishmen, but Thomas perhaps most of all. He first turned against Thomas when Thomas, with the help of Pocahontas, freed Thomas Graves, an Englishman whom Opechancanough held captive and intended to kill the next day. Later he resented Thomas's taking trade away from him and giving it to the East Shore Indians. In any case, Opechancanough ordered Ontanimo, one of his warriors, to kill Thomas. Perhaps it was this warrior who shot the arrow through Thomas's body. It didn't kill him and we don't know who shot that arrow or when it was done. Still, we do know for certain that he was shot.

By this time Thomas was probably established on the Eastern Shore and this may have been the happiest period of his life. In 1620 Thomas was 26 years old; he hadn't had much of a carefree boyhood. He had liked being an interpreter, but for the most part he had to be serious and attend to business. The people on the Eastern Shore were different; they tended to be light-hearted. And then there was Debedeavon, the Laughing King as he was called. He was warm, smiling, easy to know, ready to joke and in no time at all, he had adopted Thomas as his "son." It was not as if the Laughing King felt he was older; no, it was an affectionate term, as if he were addressing a friend. Thomas could relax around these people and be himself. As for the Indians, they accepted Thomas as one of theirs and often let him in on their councils.

One day as the Laughing King and Thomas were talking, the subject got around to running. The Laughing King must have observed with a sly smile that no white person could run as fast as an Indian. Thomas took him up on that, challenging the Laughing King to a race. They lined up as a crowd of Indians gathered. One, two, three—and they were off in their bare feet. They jogged along together for a short distance, then as they approached the finish line, they put on speed. In the end, there was no question: Thomas won. As they caught their breath, they both burst out laughing. "You would never have done it," the Laughing King said, "if you hadn't been my son." He thumped Thomas on his shoulder. "And now, Thomas Savage," he went on, "you have earned a gift for having surprised me."

The gift was 9,000 acres of uncultivated land beside the open sea—the part of the Eastern Shore that Thomas liked best.

Cultivated or not, Thomas thought, it was land! *His* land! Someday he would build a regular house on it. Not yet. Everyone on the Eastern Shore expected trouble, yes, from Opechancanough, who seemed to be waging a secret campaign to make the English believe that he loved them and was devoted to peace.

There were two people whom Opechancanough depended upon to help in his campaign. One was Nemattanew, whom the English called Jack of the Feathers because of the many feathers he had plastered on his body. Obviously he was playing the part of an Indian superman who claimed to be invulnerable. He could convince Indians of almost anything. When it was time for them to fight, he convinced them that they could win. He foretold the future. He convinced them that no English bullet could harm *him.* Clearly he possessed magic and in battle, soldiers tried to stand next to him so his magic might rub off on them.

The other man whom Opechancanough used for his purposes was a recently arrived Englishman, George Thorpe, who believed the English had used the wrong strategy with the Indians. If instead of fighting them, they would only be kind enough, they could convert the Indians and insure peace. So George Thorpe gave the Indians anything they wanted.

When the Indians complained of being frightened by the English dogs, Thorpe hanged the dogs from a tree as if they were criminals. They died in plain sight of the Indians. When Opechancanough said he'd like an English house, George Thorpe had one built for him, complete with a front door key that seemed like magic to Opechancanough. He couldn't stop locking and unlocking the door, going in and out, in and out. Opechancanough took great pains to demonstrate his friendship. Once he told George Thorpe that he'd like to know more about Christianity. Maybe the English god was more powerful than the Indian god. Still, through all this pantomime of peace, the English continued to occupy Indian land.

The people on the Eastern Shore suspected that Opechancanough was only trying to lull the English into a false sense of security. Then the time came when they not only suspected, they were sure. Opechancanough sent a messenger to the Laughing King, asking him to send a certain plant that only grew on the Eastern Shore. It was poisonous and Opechancanough, who counted the Eastern Shore Indians as his allies, explained that he planned to put the plant in the English drinking water.

The Laughing King said no, he wouldn't send the plant. He told Thomas about Opechancanough's plan and advised him to warn the governor, but the people at Jamestown trusted that Opechancanough would not break the peace he had talked so much about. They ignored the warning.

Until March 22, 1622. That was the day that Opechancanough had set for his grand massacre, the day he would force the English to leave. He would have to do this without Nemattanew, for Nemattanew, who bragged

53

that no English bullet would kill him, had been killed by an English bullet. Before he died, Nemattanew asked to be buried with the English. The Indians need not know that his magic had failed.

Magic or not, Opechancanough proceeded with his plan. He had prepared the Indians in the area to act as if it were a normal day. They should visit homes where they had been welcomed. They were to carry no weapons; instead they were to grab English weapons and start killing. When they came to George Thorpe, it wasn't enough to kill him once. They attacked him with scalping knives, swords, hatchets, axes—first the living body, then the dead one. At the end of the day, after killing 347 English, they reported to Opechancanough.

Had the remaining English surrendered and left? Opechancanough wanted to know.

No, they showed no signs of leaving.

Then they'd have to do this again, Opechancanough said. He didn't know when, but everyone, including the English, knew that Opechancanough's hatchet would fall another time. Meanwhile, the English prepared for additional colonists to arrive, claimed the territory that Indians considered theirs and sought revenge.

While everyone was waiting for Opechancanough to take up his hatchet, Thomas decided that this was a good time to build his house. Perhaps it seemed to him that if he built it now, he would also be making a statement. No matter what happened, he was saying that he was staying. Virginia was his home. His house was built to withstand time and attack. Since the house has not survived to modern times, we have only a hearsay description. Doors were supposedly three inches thick; handmade locks were twelve by eight

inches and an inch thick. Stone steps were imported from England and furniture was delivered directly by a sailing schooner. The house must have been close to the water, probably for the convenience of his own boats.

There was another reason Thomas might have wanted the house. This was 1624 (Thomas was 30 years old) and a new census had been issued on the colony. Jamestown was listed with a population of 1,200 (which increased in the next ten years to 5,200). The names of individuals living in the colony were included. Under *S*, it read: "Savage, Thomas, gentleman." Well, how could he be anything else? With all that land he had been given! According to the census, he had a house, a barn, a boat and two indentured servants.

He must have felt satisfaction in becoming a gentleman after all this time, but perhaps he wasn't quite as pleased as he might have once expected. "Gentleman" didn't mean as much or describe him as well as "interpreter," which implied a life of activity and put him in the center of the government's business.

It was also time, Thomas decided, to acquire a wife. Although there weren't many young women to choose from, there was one: Ann (or Hannah) Tyng, who had come to Jamestown several years ago on a ship with Ralph Hamor. Hamor had, of course, worked with Thomas and may have introduced the two to each other. In any case, after he had met Ann Tyng, Thomas decided she'd *do*. And Ann thought she couldn't do any better than Thomas, who already had a house. So they settled down and in a short time, they had a son, John, who looked like Thomas and had the same quiet disposition.

This might have been a happy time for the Savage family except for one thing. William Eppes was made commander of the company lands that adjoined Thomas's property. Eppes was a hotheaded man with a reputation for brawling, so it was no wonder that Thomas was concerned when he became his neighbor. Up to his old tricks, Eppes was soon picking a fight with Thomas, accusing Thomas of having slandered him. He visited Thomas's house and confronted him with his words.

And what had Thomas said to bring this on? He was in fear of his life, he had said, because of Eppes.

We can only guess that Thomas tried to calm Eppes, but Eppes was not easily calmed. As usual he took it upon himself to make Thomas regret what he'd said. He tied his feet around his neck, a painful punishment to endure but, as the only observer present remarked, "Thomas spoke no bad language throughout."

Still, Eppes was not through with Thomas. The next step was to bring Thomas before Sir George Yeardley, the governor, who was also a good friend of William Eppes. Thomas was duly convicted of slander and insubordination. The punishment? Thomas was to do any interpreting that either Yeardley or Eppes desired. Since Thomas was known for being successful in getting land grants and supplies of corn, he was much in demand as an interpreter. His punishment obviously favored his accuser, but whether Thomas was bound exclusively to Yeardley's and Eppes's service is not known. In any case, in 1627 Yeardley died and Eppes moved to the West Indies, so Thomas was on his own. In addition to interpreting, he worked to make the Eastern Shore a center for valuable fur trading.

Opechancanough did not take up his hatchet again until 1644. He was an old, old man now—nearly 100 years old, some said.

He could not walk alone. He could not open his own eyes; someone else had to prop them open for him. He could still kill, but he could not chase away a whole colony. In April 1644, Opechancanough arranged an attack that killed nearly 500 English.

In the end, Opechancanough was captured and taken to the Jamestown prison, where he was shot in the back by a prison guard.

Thomas was not there for Opechancanough's last act. Thomas Savage had died in 1635; he was 41 years old. He would not have been worried that Opechancanough might drive the English out. There were too many English now (8,000) and they were not easily discouraged. Thomas was proud of his colony and its success. At the same time, he found it hard to watch the Indians retreating and retreating. He supposed that one day, even the Laughing King would have to go.

Thomas didn't talk or write about his experiences. Nor about himself. We have to depend on what other people said. John Pory, secretary of the Jamestown Colony, who once worked with Thomas, had this to say:

"He, with much honesty and good successe, served the publique without any publique recognition, yet had an arrow shot through his body in their service." These words, along with the following description of his services, were transferred three hundred years later to a plaque and hung on the wall of the Old Jamestown Church.

> *Thomas Savage, Gentleman and Ensign, the first white settler on the Eastern Shore of Virginia. Hostage to Powhatan, 1608; his loyalty and fearlessness endeared him to the great king who treated him as his son. While he rendered invaluable aid to the colony as interpreter, greatly beloved by Debedeavon, The Laughing King of the Accawmackes, he was given a tract of nine thousand acres of land known as Savage's Neck. He obtained food for the starving colony at Jamestown through his friendship with the kindly Eastern Shore Indians.*

These words are still there.
As they should be.

NOTES

Page 6 · "He was thirteen years old and perhaps an orphan."

Although various sources give ages that differ by a year or two, I have chosen thirteen since that seems to be used most often. To my knowledge, there is no source that claims Thomas was an orphan. There is, however, no mention of a mother or father, so the "orphan" may or may not be factual. He may have been so far down the line in a large family that he knew he would inherit nothing. His parents may have allowed him to shift for himself.

There is also no contemporary reference to his being a "cabin boy," but he is so often called a "cabin boy" that I chose to consider it, if not true, certainly likely.

Page 6 · "Where there were spiders, there was gold."

This was a folk belief widely held in the sixteenth century.

Page 38 · "New Style calendar"

Up until 1582, the Gregorian calendar had been followed with every month having the same number of days, but at the end of the year there was always time left over and no one knew what to do with it. In 1582 the Pope fixed that. He introduced the Julian calendar. Some months had 30 days; some had 31. February had only 28 but every four years (leap year) it had 29. For a long time people added NS to a date if it was figured on the new calendar; OS if it was figured on the old.

Page 46 · Powhatan's speech to Thomas is still in its original form, reported by Frederick Fausz, "Middlemen in Peace and War," *The Virginia Magazine of History and Biography*, January 1987.

Page 50 · Another name that the Laughing King used, perhaps for formal occasions, was Esme Shichans.

"The legend is that Savage won the land in a foot race with the Laughing King." August Burghard, *America's First Family*, p. 60.

Pages 54–55 · There is no firsthand description of Thomas's house from his time. The description used is hearsay. It can be found in August Burghard's book *America's First Family*, p. 69.

Page 57 · Thomas's expression of fear over what Eppes might do is the only direct quotation we have from Thomas.

BIBLIOGRAPHY

ANDREWS, K. R. "Christopher Newport of Limehouse, Mariner." *The William and Mary Quarterly*, third series, 11 (January 1954): 28–41.

BARBOUR, PHILIP. *The Three Worlds of Captain John Smith*. Boston: Houghton Mifflin, 1964.

BILLINGS, WARREN M. *The Old Dominion in the Seventeenth Century*. Chapel Hill: University of North Carolina Press, 1975.

BRIDENBAGH, CARL. *Vexed and Troubled Englishmen, 1590–1642*. New York: Oxford University Press, 1968.

———. *Early Americans*. New York: Oxford University Press, 1981.

———. *Jamestown, 1544–1699*. New York: Oxford University Press, 1980.

BROWN, ALEXANDER. *The Genesis of the United States*. New York: Russell & Russell, 1964.

BURGHARD, AUGUST. *America's First Family, the Savages of Virginia*. Philadelphia: Dorrance, 1974.

FAUSZ, J. FREDERICK. "Middlemen in Peace and War: Virginia's Earliest Indian Interpreters, 1608–1632." *The Virginia Magazine of History and Biography* 95 (January 1987): 41–64.

HAILE, EDWARD WRIGHT, ed. *Jamestown Narratives*. Champlain, Va.: Roundhouse, 1998.

KATZ, STANLEY N., JOHN M. MURRIN, AND DOUGLAS GREENBERG, eds. *Colonial America: Essays in Politics and Social Development*. 4th ed. New York: McGraw-Hill, 1993.

KINGSBURY, SUSAN MYRA, ed. *The Record of the Virginia Company of London*. 4 vols. Washington, D.C.: U.S. Government Printing Office, 1906–1935.

LARSON, R.K.T. "Thomas Savage—Cabin Boy." *The Richmonden Magazine*, May 1931.

POWELL, WILLIAM STEVENS. "John Pory 1572–1636." *Virginia Cavalcade*, Summer 1968.

PRICE, DAVID A. *Love & Hate in Jamestown*. New York: Alfred A. Knopf, 2003.

ROUNTREE, HELEN E. *The Powhatan Indians of Virginia*. Norman: University of Oklahoma Press, 1989.

———. *Pocahontas, Powhatan, Opechancanough*. Charlottesville: University of Virginia Press, 2005.

SAVAGE-ARMSTRONG, GEORGE FRANCIS. *The Ancient and Noble Family of the Savages of the Ards*. London: M. Ward & Co., 1888.

SMITH, BRADFORD. *Captain John Smith, His Life and Legend*. New York: Lippincott, 1953.

STEPHENS, SIR ROBERT, AND SIR LEE SIDNEYS, eds. *The Dictionary of National Biography*. Vol. XIV. London: Oxford University Press, 1954.

STILES, MARTHA BENNETT. "Hostage to the Indians." *Virginia Cavalcade*, Summer 1962.

THOMAS, PHILLIP FARRINGTON. *Personal Links: The Odyssey of an Extended American Family*. Manuscript copyright 2004 by Phillip Thomas.

WISE, JENNINGS CROPPER. *Ye Kingdome of Accawmacke, or, The Eastern Shore of Virginia in the Seventeenth Century*. Richmond, Va.: Bell Book and Stationery Co., 1911.

INDEX